To Kaili Jo
Reach high

MW00878605

Making the
GRADE

Ricky L. Coston Jr., M.Ed., NCC

Ricky L. Coston Jr.

Making the Grade

Copyright © 2018 by Ricky L. Coston Jr.
Cover design Copyright © 2018 by Ricky L. Coston Jr.

All rights reserved. This book or any portion thereof may not be reproduced or used in any manner whatsoever without the express written permission of the publisher except for the use of brief quotations in a book review.

First edition published 2018.
Printed in the United States of America

ISBN-13: 978-1724849762
ISBN-10: 172484976X

ABOUT THE AUTHOR

First and foremost, I would like to thank you for taking a look at this book. Before you read any further, I would like to introduce myself to you, explain what influenced me to write this book, and share what I would like for you to receive from this book. Please feel free to reach out to me if you have any questions, comments, or would like to discuss anything further.

Well, you can't have an introduction without giving your name. Hello, Reader. My name is Ricky Coston. Many people think my name is short for Richard, but it's actually Ricky. I grew up in a small town in Virginia called Dunnsville. I attended and graduated at the top of my class in the Essex County Public Schools system which is located in Tappahannock, Virginia. I'm not trying to brag about myself, but I would like for you to get to know me a little. So, while in school, I had many friends but my love for learning was indeed a priority. The expression "keep your head" in the books was indeed a major part of my life. From elementary school to high school, the first thing that I always did after getting home from school was my homework. After that, I would read a book, relax, play some video games, or watch some tv. Of course as I became older, I found time for friends, sports, and other extracurricular activities. I was involved in baseball, track, tennis, cross country, debate, Odyssey of the Mind, academic challenge, the National Honor Society, and several activities at my church. All of these activities, along with my academic success, allowed me to go to the college of my dreams on a full-ride scholarship. Yes, I am a graduate of The College of William and Mary.

I originally went to William and Mary because when I was in the seventh grade, I made my mind up that I would go to William and Mary and become a lawyer. This was a desire that I had and used to stay motivated while in high school. After I started my undergraduate career at William and Mary, I double majored in psychology and philosophy. I figured these two majors would be the most beneficial for my career as a lawyer. On the one hand, I could learn how people think, and on the other hand, I could learn how to outthink them. But, as I got closer and closer to my graduation date, I began to speak to God more and more. Oh yeah, did I mention that I became a deacon at Good Hope Baptist Church (my home church in Dunnsville) when I was 21. So, I changed my mind which had it been made up for several years, and I decided to become a school counselor. I decided that I wanted to help people before they needed help in court. What better place than in a school where their minds are already being molded. Plus, everyone goes to school, so I would have hundreds and hundreds of opportunities to help people and change the world one student at a time. To this day, I believe this is one purpose in my life.

So, I received my Bachelors of Arts in Psychology and in Philosophy in May 2012. A few months later, I began my coursework at William and Mary again, but this time, it was to receive my Masters of Education in School Counseling. This coursework continued to shape my life beyond what I had previously experienced during my undergraduate years. I learned counseling techniques and theories, but I also learned even more about myself and my self-evaluation became more profound. My perception of myself, the world, and the people in it continued to evolve. In May 2014, at the age of 24, I received my Masters and a few months later, I received my certification as a Nationally Certified Counselor. A short time later, in August 2014, I began working as a Professional School Counselor for Manassas Park City Schools in Manassas Park, Virginia. I've only been working as a Professional School Counselor for a few years, but I have learned so much along the way. I'm thankful for the knowledge that I obtained from my coursework, but I am even more thankful for the experiences that I have shared with my school staff and each of my students.

The purpose of this book is to reach the students and young adults that I am unable to see face to face in my office. I have had the pleasure of working with students between the ages of 4 and 21. I primarily work with elementary students, but there are high school and middle school students that continue to reach out to me for guidance and assistance. Knowing that you are sought out to assist someone on their life journey is a feeling that's more than amazing. It is a blessing in itself.

Throughout my life, and even to this day, I have been influenced by role models and people that truly care about me. Besides God, my family is the biggest source of influence in my life, especially my mom. I grew up living with my mom and my sister. My mom is without a doubt the strongest and most altruistic person I know. She is a private contractor, and she goes out of her way to help anyone in need, especially her family and the elderly. I learned so many things from my mom including the value of hard work and the importance of caring for other people. I still remember helping her chop down trees and split wood for my grandma and the elderly that needed wood for the winter. And during the summer, we used to cut grass and trim bushes for the elderly that were unable to do it themselves. My mom has definitely been one of my top role models and someone that I still look up to today. She still cuts my hair and helps me out with my vehicle repairs. I love my mom. My sister is on the autism spectrum. Growing up with her had its challenges. We fought a lot and just had a hard time seeing eye-to-eye. She always got on my nerves. But, overtime I started to understand her more and I developed more and more patience towards her. There were many things that I taught her during our childhood, such as how to hit and catch a baseball, how to play video games (we still do that from time to time), and how to "run fast" (her words not mine) for her Special Olympics track events held each year. She still asks me every year to help her practice for her events. Now even though I taught her many things, she has taught me just as much. The most valuable thing that my sister taught me was empathy. Putting yourself in the shoes of another person to see their perspectives allows you to understand them deeper and maybe even respect them more. As a Professional School Counselor who subscribes to Person-Centered and Solution

Focused counseling theories, empathy is a skill that drives my practice. I have to thank my sister for that. In fact, I thought about my sister and our life together when I decided to pursue a career as a Professional School Counselor. I love my sister. Even though I lived with my mom and sister, my dad was another huge part of my life. He is a JROTC Instructor, and he was always there for us in more ways than just financially. He visited us often and through those experiences, he taught me the value of making time to be with others. I remember going fishing with my dad from time to time and just talking about life. I always looked forward to those moments with him. We still have those moments to this day. Along with my mom, my dad taught me a lot of skills that I still use. The best thing that my dad taught and modeled for me, is how to take a step back and remain calm. I love my dad.

Once again, thank you for getting to know me and for taking a look at this book. Please know that this book may not have all of the answers in life that you are looking for. Instead, let it provoke some thoughts and provide a guide that you can use to further your development as the best person that you are meant to be. I hope that you participate in the exercises that are described in the later chapters as they can help provide various benefits. Happy reading and growing!

This book is dedicated to all of those who have made a difference in my life. I hope to do the same for many others. To my family, friends, and especially Brianna... thank you.

CHAPTER 1

What is Your Profile?

This chapter is all about finding your identity. It seems like a good place to start because you have to have some idea of yourself before you can appreciate anything else. Notice that I said "have some of idea yourself" instead of saying "know yourself completely." I chose to use these words because you will find that your identity will continue to change over time. You will continue to find out new things about yourself. Your appearance, likes and dislikes, friendships, interests, knowledge, and even your beliefs will continue to change over time. Let me give you some quick examples: Years ago, you spent every day in diapers without a care in the world. Your interests included exploring and discovering new things, eating, napping, and gaining attention from everyone. You believed that everything was yours and that everything was meant to either be played with or eaten. Some years after that, hopefully no longer in diapers, you were in elementary school learning math, reading and language arts, history, and science. Your interests included making new friends, having fun, television, and other things that caught your interest. You may have believed in things such as the importance of tattling, being first in line, having special responsibilities, being heard, and being the best. These are just a few examples. However, what is your identity right now?

Let's pause for a moment and make a quick clarification. Now, you may be thinking to yourself "if I am going to change into a different person later, why does it matter who I am or what I do now." Well, it matters…a lot. It is very important to know that what you do now, will have an effect on you later. As you get older, you will see that you can learn from your past, but you can't escape your past. Let me give you two examples from my own life:

1. One day, when I was a kid, I was watching a cartoon episode of Superman. He was fighting crime, flying through the air, and just being Superman. I wanted to be like him so much! So, I climbed onto the couch and decided to fly to the other side of the room. I leaped from the couch and…the next thing I remember, I was in a hospital getting stitches in my forehead and eating a chocolate tootsie roll pop. I don't remember jumping head first into the coffee table. I remember the beginning and end of this story, but my mom had to tell me the middle. There were two things that I learned that night: 1) look before you leap and 2) leave the flying to superheroes. Now, this moment in my past will always be a part of me, along with the permanent scar on my forehead. You may have a similar story.

2. While I was in school, I made good grades and I did a lot of extracurricular activities. I did track, tennis, cross country, academic challenge, debate, Odyssey of the Mind, and I was a member of the National Honor Society. Also, while I was in school, I took advanced courses offered at my high school,

I took dual-enrollment courses at the community college, and I was a student at the Chesapeake Bay Governor's School (a program offered at Rappahannock Community College that recruits the top students from the surrounding school districts). Due to all of my hard work, and with the support of my family and friends, I was admitted to The College of William and Mary. Not only that, I was admitted on a full-ride scholarship. I spent the next four years enjoying a great college experience without having to pay a single penny. In fact, I always had extra money after all of my expenses were paid. So when you think about it, I was paid every year to go to college. I am truly grateful for my college experience, because it shaped the life that I am living today. I grew so much as an individual over the course of those four years, and there were so many things that I discovered about myself. I gained new interests, acquired more knowledge, met many new friends, and developed new ways of looking at life. Still, it is all thanks to my work in elementary, middle, and high school. Hard work paid off for me, and it can pay off for you, too.

The past does make a difference. I hope you can recall similar examples in your own life. Most importantly, I hope you see that your actions now CAN and WILL have an impact on you later in your life. One experience leads to the next.

What is your profile? Your profile can be divided into two categories. The first one is similar to Facebook. WHAT DOES

EVERYONE KNOW ABOUT YOU? This can cover a wide range of things: hobbies, interests, actions, likes, dislikes, and anything that other people know about you whether you want them to know it or not. There is a difference between knowing something and thinking you know something. Sometimes other people will think they know something about you, but it could be wrong. When this happens, you can do two things: you can either calmly confront the other person (never resort to violence, threats, name calling, or escalating a situation) or ignore that person. That is why the second category is the most important. WHAT DO YOU KNOW ABOUT YOURSELF? This category includes what you know and what everyone else may know. What you know to be true about yourself is what's most important.

Now, if you focus on "what do you know about yourself," well…what do you know about yourself? I'm sure you can create an entire list of information about yourself concerning your physical attributes, hobbies, religious beliefs, favorites, relationships/friendships, and so on and so on. However, don't forget that your identity will change over time. As your profile gets updated, you will see that some things will get replaced, added, and removed. Besides these changes that will occur, here is something else that may shock you:

YOU ONLY KNOW YOURSELF ON THE SURFACE LEVEL.

Surface level? What does that mean? You are more complex than you think. The older that you get, the more complex you will become. This is because your reasoning and intuitive skills will become more enhanced and your critical eye will become sharper. But even now, I'm sure that you are more complex than you think. In order to see how complex you actually are, you must look past the surface level. How do you do that? *REFLECTIONS.*

A reflection is a process where an individual observes and explores something in order to gain a deeper understanding. In simple terms, it means taking the time to either look back on something or to look at something that is occurring right now. In a reflection, you can explore the who, what, where, when, why, and how in any situation. Why did this happen, why did I feel this way when that happened, who is getting on my nerves, why is this getting to me, why do I like this instead of that, how am I doing in this situation, what is my goal and what am I doing to achieve that goal, where am I heading, where is my problem occurring the most, what do I want to do with my life, and where do I want to go after I graduate from school? You can reflect on anything. You can reflect on good situations, bad situations, personal things, memories, past events, relationships, friendships, thoughts about the future, and anything that comes to mind. Let me give an example where a person uses time to reflect in order to learn something about themselves:

Mike is a sophomore at his high school. His grades are pretty good and he enjoys hanging out with his friends. Mike doesn't participate in any extracurricular activities even though he does feel the need to do something. Mike realizes that he does watch a lot of movies. In fact, Mike spends so much time watching movies that he begins to notice different aspects that he had never noticed before. He begins to look at the dialogue between the actors and their movements. This starts to become a hobby for him. Here is his reflection:

Instead of going out to the movies, I decided to stay in and watch one. Tonight, I watched "John Q." Denzel Washington is THE MAN! I mean he just makes everything look good. His facial expressions, actions, and dialogue seem to fit everything perfectly. This character could not have been played any better. I wish I could do something like that. Must be cool to be famous like that. Wish I was rich like that, too. I don't know why I'm spending so much time watching these actors in these movies and wishing for something that isn't going to happen. But, it does make me feel good when I watch these movies. And it would be cool to do something like that. It's whatever though because I can't do something like that. I'm way too shy. It would be great if I can get over my shyness, but I don't know if I can. I thought about joining the theatre club. It seems alright and I could be doing something after school. But, I'm still shy...I think I'm going to try it anyway. I don't have anything to lose.

After some time reflecting on this new hobby, Mike learned that he is very interested in acting. It explains why he is interested in his observations and why he feels good when he watches movies. But there is a problem. Mike is shy. Still, he decides to challenge himself by overcoming his shyness and joining the theatre club. Mike is now a junior in high school with the lead role in the upcoming school play. Here is another example:

Brittany is a freshman at her high school. Heather is Brittany's best friend. They have been really close for a few years now. A few weeks ago, Heather made a comment that hurt Brittany's feelings. Trying not to make a big deal out of it, Brittany tried to forget what happened. Recently, Brittany was reminded about what happened a few weeks ago. She realized that she never got over it. Here is her reflection:

> *I hung out with Heather again today. Everything was going fine until she called me fat again. It sounded like she was joking when she said it. So I'm sure she didn't mean. She did the same thing like two weeks ago. I tried to forget about it because it probably doesn't mean anything. She does stuff like this all of the time. It hurts my feelings a little but it's no big deal. I know she's my best friend and wouldn't do anything to hurt me on purpose. It would be nice if she didn't do that though. Maybe I'm starting to make a big deal out of nothing.*

But, it's not just Heather. Other people do the same thing to me. I just want everyone to see me as a good friend. Is it my fault for letting them walk over me like that? I think I'm starting to make a big deal out of this. But, I don't like letting my feelings get hurt. If I say something to Heather or to some of the other people, things might get awkward and they may not want to be friends with me anymore because they might think I let stuff get to me too much. But, if Heather is my best friend, then I think she should be able to understand where I'm coming from. I think I'm going to talk to her about it.

After some time to reflect on this situation, Brittany realized that this problem has occurred many times in her friendship with Heather. Brittany learned that she usually gets her feelings hurt by Heather and avoids doing anything about it. Brittany learned that she spends more time trying to please other people instead of looking out for herself. She fears losing a friend if she makes a big deal out of a situation. Brittany decides that it is time to overcome her fear. She calmly confronts Heather. Now, their friendship is better than ever. Brittany has even become more assertive in other aspects of her life.

These are just two examples of the good that can come from reflecting. But sometimes a reflection can bring up something that may be unpleasant. Let's look back at the previous example that involves Brittany. It may have been unpleasant for her to learn that she usually let's Heather mistreat her. In times like these, it is important to know that the more you know about yourself, the more you are able to grow. Even though this realization may have been unpleasant for Brittany, she was able to take what she learned and turn it into something positive. She overcame her fear and she is no longer a pushover. She cares more about herself and her actions now show it. Notice that in both of these examples, the person did something to challenge themselves. Challenges and confrontations helped each of them grow. Sometimes a reflection can lead the reflector to try something new, continue something, replace something, or stop something. In any case, reflecting can lead to growth.

I challenge you to participate in reflection exercises. Start out with spending time reflecting on situations as they occur. Later, spend a set amount of time (maybe five or ten minutes) once a week reflecting on any topic that you want. For example, you can reflect on how you feel about some aspect of your life (grades, school, future, hobby, extracurricular activities, friendships, goals, etc.). You can even reflect on what is happening in the world. Write everything down in a journal so that you can keep track of your thoughts and reflections. After some time has passed (days, weeks, or months), go back and read over your reflections. Pay attention to your thoughts, feelings, and ideas as you look over what you have written. This may lead you to reflect on that experience of reading what you wrote.

I know that this may sound like work, and you may already have enough work to do. But trust me, this will become an enjoyable experience, you will learn some things about yourself, and you will continue to grow along the way.

Here is a list of topics that you can reflect on (but don't just stop here, come up with your own ideas):

- What is my favorite thing to do and why
- I consider _____ to be my friend because…
- I believe a best friend is…
- Today, _____(this event)_____ happened. It made me feel/think about…
- I am really good at…
- I want to get better at _____ because…
- I think I should work on ____(this aspect about myself)____ because…
- I wish I could replace _____ with _____. (this can be activities, interests, people, ideas, or anything)
- I think I am _____ because of _____. (can be anything)

Final Words

Nobody knows you like you know you, and there is more of you that you should get to know. Love yourself, know yourself, and make yourself proud. Live YOUR life. YOU are in CONTROL of YOUR LIFE.

CHAPTER 2

A Picture is Worth More Than a Thousand Words

What you do and how you look says a lot about you. This chapter is about your appearance. I'm not talking about your natural appearance. Instead, I'm talking about how you display yourself. This includes clothes, make-up, tattoos, jewelry, your actions, what you say, and anything else that other people see when they see you.

Actually, let's take a minute to talk about natural appearance. Natural appearance is a person without their jewelry, make-up, or anything that they wear or place on their body. It is all of the characteristics of their bare body. Basic psychology tells us that the people who are judged to be attractive tend to get treated better than those who are not said to be attractive. I'm sure you have already seen this in your life. The cool and popular people are handsome, cute, gorgeous, pretty, and so on and so on. When a person is judged to be physically ugly, they tend to be treated poorly by others.

I'm going to give you my philosophy on natural appearance. You can take it or leave it, but please consider it:

1. If you are a beautiful person, then you should be respected instead of mistreated.

2. In terms of natural appearance, all people are beautiful because they are beautifully created and they beautifully exist in this world.

3. Therefore, EVERYONE should be respected instead of mistreated because they are beautifully created.

In a world where every single person should be equal, shouldn't everyone be judged to be beautiful?

Based on my philosophy, there is a difference between thinking someone is beautiful and thinking someone is physically attractive. Like I said, all people are beautiful. But when you think someone is physically attractive, it means that you would like to be in a relationship with that person...or at least you wouldn't mind being more than just friends. Okay...moving on. For now, let's focus on how you display yourself. We will begin with your outside appearance.

What you say on the outside is usually what you are saying on the inside. What does that mean? Your physical appearance is a reflection of your personality, what you think about yourself, and what you want other people to think about you. Your outside physical appearance is a combination of what you look like, what you say, and what you do.

If you were to look in the mirror, what would you see? Not only will you see your beautiful natural appearance, you will also see what other people see when they look at you. NEWSFLASH, people are judged based on what they wear. When I say "what you wear" I mean your clothes, jewelry, make-up, and HOW you wear all of this stuff. If you look like you have a lazy appearance, other people will think you have a lazy personality. If you have a provocative appearance, other people will think you have a provocative personality. If you look like a bum or a thug, other people will associate you with the characteristics of these types of people. If you look studious, then other people will think you are studious. If you look like a professional, then other people will associate you with the characteristics of a professional. What do you want other people to see when they look at you? Do you want them to see a person who respects and cares about him or herself, or would you rather them see you as a person who doesn't care about him or herself?

It is worth saying that psychology experiments show that humans tend to make judgments of other people in less than five seconds. This is usually based on physical appearance, but it can also involve how a person acts, speaks, and conducts themselves. One of the reasons why these fast judgments are made is because at an early age, and as people go through life, they develop classification systems known as schemas. I don't want to bore you with the details, so I will keep it short. People learn different stereotypes and they can use these stereotypes to classify other people in less than five seconds. Think of it this way. There are stereotypes for different types of people, what they may do for a living, and how they interact with other people. You may not want to be judged by other people before they actually get to know you, but all of this furthers the idea of focusing on your appearance and making a good impression.

Now, that we are done talking about what other people see and think about you, let's talk about how you see yourself. When you look in the mirror, what do you see? I hope that if you are a boy, you see someone that is handsome, and if you are a girl, you see someone that is gorgeous. People who see themselves this way tend to be more confident and have higher self-esteem. They believe that they can do anything. I hope you can see your natural attractiveness.

Unfortunately, there may be times where you may have a hard time seeing the beauty in yourself. Maybe it's because you are having a bad day, maybe it's because you are lacking some confidence, or maybe it's because you actually believe that you are not attractive at all. In any case, it's something that needs to be addressed. You should find the beauty in you to appreciate two things: the beauty in this world and your ability to do anything in this beautiful world.

I challenge you to do an exercise every day. Set aside five minutes each day to look in a mirror and find at least one thing that you like about yourself physically. It can be anything… even something as small as your pinky toe. With this exercise it is best to focus on a specific characteristic. Really take the time to appreciate your true physical beauty. Say out loud what it is that you like about yourself physically and why. Then, take the time to find at least one thing that you like about yourself internally. When I say internally, I am referring to your characteristics that may not be seen on your body physically. Instead, they can refer to your actions, how you conduct yourself, and your personality. Maybe you like how confident you are. Maybe you like how respectful you are. Maybe you like how dedicated you are towards what's important to you. You should acknowledge these characteristics because they make up you, too.

But what if you have a hard time finding something that you like about yourself? Well instead of spending five minutes on this exercise, spend ten minutes. I know it sounds crazy, but it can help you if you truly try it. In those cases, start small and work your way up. Find a small body part or a small feature that you like. Why do you like it? Why is it attractive? Is it one of your best features? These are the types of questions that you should be answering. Now, why should you do this each day? Again, you should find the beauty in you to appreciate two things: the beauty in this world and your ability to do anything in this beautiful world.

Build up your confidence by finding those physical features. After that, take a look at your internal features. We spent a lot of time talking about how you look physically. But, you should also take a look at everything else that makes up YOU.

What makes you beautiful?
- Physically   _____
- Internally   _____

Final Words

A healthy and natural you is the most beautiful you that you can be. Treat your body right because it was the one and only body that was given to you at birth. Stay fit, exercise, eat healthy, and take care of your beautiful and natural self. Appreciate your true beauty both inside and out. While you appreciate your own true beauty, appreciate the beauty of others and the world.

CHAPTER 3

Flex Your Strengths

In this chapter, I will discuss how strong you are. No, I'm not talking about how much you can bench press or lift. As far as I know, maybe you are super strong and can lift a ton. Instead, I'm talking about the things that you are good at and the things that make you stand out from everyone else. What makes you awesome, unique, special, and cool? These are your gifts, your talents and your strengths.

Everyone is good at something even if you think that something is small. In other words, everyone has a gift. Whether you are gifted in being really smart or super athletic, there is something that makes you outstanding. Your gift may also be your kindness and the ability to make many friends. No matter what your gift may be, it should be something that makes you proud and strong.

But what if you are having a hard time finding out your gifts? What if you feel like you aren't good at anything? Well, you can do a few things in this case. One, you can believe that you aren't good at anything, give up, and feel worthless. Or two, you can believe that there is at least one thing that you are good at, keep trying, and feel priceless. Even if you haven't found that one thing that you are proud of, you should keep searching until you do. Your strength may be something that develops over time. Try new things and find who you are and what you like to do. Or in fact, I am willing to bet that you have already found it but haven't quite realized it yet. If this is the case, here are a few questions that may help you realize your hidden strength:

1. Is there anything that is really easy for you to do?
2. Have your friends said that you are really good at something?
3. Is there anything that you really enjoy doing?

Now, there are three more items in regards to that last question. First, there could be something that you really enjoy doing and you consider it one of your talents. Second, there could be something that you really enjoy doing and you don't consider it a talent because it's not something that you would consider a major talent or a big deal. In other words, you may think it is small, minor, and everyone can do it. Third, there could be something that you really enjoy doing but you don't think that you are either good at it or good enough at it. In any of these situations, remember two ideas…BE PROUD OF YOURSELF AND NEVER STOP IMPROVING YOURSELF!

One of the best things that you can do for yourself is to be proud of yourself. When this happens, you stay motivated, you feel like you are on top of the world, and you start to find even more things about yourself to be proud of and appreciate. It's like a ripple effect. One thing leads to another which leads to another.

Now what if you still feel like that one thing that you enjoy is not something to be majorly proud of because many other people can do the same thing. Well, even though that may be true, you can still make this YOUR UNIQUE TALENT by putting YOUR OWN SPIN on it. Let me give you a few examples. In the game of basketball, many people do slam dunks. But some people have gone above and beyond by creating and performing different and unique slam dunks that really get the crowds hype. Here's another example…if you enjoy making friends, maybe it's because of the unique way that you make friends and that draws them to you. Here's another example…maybe you enjoy making peanut butter and jelly sandwiches. True, what kind of example is this? Many people can make PB&J sandwiches, but no one can make them like you. Do you put peanut butter on one slice of bread and jelly on the other? Do you use three slices of bread? Do you use twice as much peanut butter? Do you mix the peanut butter and jelly? Creamy or chunky peanut butter? THAT is the key here. No, not the peanut butter. I say all of this to say that even the really common things that many people can do…NOBODY CAN DO IT QUITE LIKE YOU. Make it your own. Be your own unique self.

Maybe you enjoy something because you are good at it. Instead of being good at it, be great at it. Many times when people are in a competition, they are competing against another person. HOWEVER, I am challenging you to compete more against yourself than anybody else. Let me give you two scenarios for why I say that:

1. Let's say you aren't the best at something and will never truly be the best at it. Actually, there's a saying that there is always someone better at something than you. Now, if you aren't the best at something, should that keep you from getting better at it? Shouldn't you continue to enjoy it and try to be the best that you can at it? Yes.

2. Let's say that in the entire world you are the best at something. No one will ever be as good at it as you. So…now what? Do you stop because you already reached the top? Sounds pretty boring. Shouldn't you keep trying to be even better at it? Even if you are better than other people at something, that shouldn't be enough. Keep getting better.

The key is not being better than other people. The key is being YOUR best. You will not achieve your best until you continue to challenge yourself and get better and better. Still, maybe you are only motivated by competing against other people. Now, you can be motivated by competing against someone else to better yourself. Who knows, you may even break and set a record. But remember this, records are broken all of the time. So even though you may set a record, someone else can come along and break it. Records are meant to be broken but your motivation should not. So, I challenge you to keep getting better and better at whatever it is that you want to do. Always work towards your best.

Flex your strengths and let them outshine your weaknesses. This does not mean to neglect or forget about your weaknesses. We must remember that no one is perfect, but we can always work towards perfection. That is done by focusing on our strengths and strengthening our weaknesses. If you flex one of your strengths hard enough, you may turn it into a career. People who have careers instead of jobs are those people who are great at what they do, love it, and can't imagine working anywhere else or doing anything else. These are the people that have put a lot of work into flexing their strengths. These are the people who tend to be extremely successful with their lives. You may see them on television as actors, athletes, singers, or other celebrities. Whether they are one of the major celebrities or the person that no one has heard of yet, they are happy because they are doing what they truly want to do.

I train in Shotokan Karate (amongst various other martial arts). Shotokan Karate is a traditional martial arts that originated from Okinawa, which is found in Japan. This martial arts relies heavily on tradition and a special code that we call our "dojo kun." It is a motto that we strive to live by each day. Each line is significant and has an in-depth meaning that has been taught to us by the original masters of this martial art. But to keep a long story short, we are reminded through this motto to keep training, never give up, and treat others with respect.

Japanese Version

Jinkaku kansei ni tsutomuru koto

Makoto no michi o mamoru koto

Doryoku no seishin o yashinau koto

Reigi o omonzuru koto

Keki no yu o imashimuru koto

English Version

Seek perfection of character

Be faithful

Endeavor

Respect others

Refrain from violent behavior

Final Words

No matter what you do, do the best that you can and never stop. Never stop can mean doing it until you can't do it anymore. And when you reach a high level, spread your knowledge to others so that they can grow and continue to share the knowledge that you bestowed upon them. This not only makes you grow stronger, but it can also make you legendary.

I leave you with two questions:

1. What are you good at?
2. What do you want to do?

CHAPTER 4

Bounce Back, Move Forward

Every day, people are faced with challenges, stressors, and things that make them upset. Nobody has a perfect life where everything goes there way every single day. This is true even for people who seem to have an easy life because they are wealthy. So, when things don't go your way, what are you going to do? This chapter is about one word…RESILIENCE.

What is resilience? In a nutshell…bounce back, move forward. Get up and keep going. Shake off the bad and focus on the good. Have you ever gotten upset because someone said or did something to you that you didn't like? Have you ever gotten your feelings hurt? Have you ever lost at something or didn't do as well as you may have wanted to do? Did something just not go your way? All people have gone through at least one of these hardships before. But what happened afterwards? Did you give up? Did you quit and never try again? Did you wish that you had never tried at all? Did you want to get revenge? Did you want to run away from that person or thing that brought you down? Well, if you are a person that did give up, wished that you had never tried, or just ran away, I bet you didn't feel good about yourself or the outcome. If you are this type of person, then your level of resilience could use a boost. So, how can you boost your resilience? First, let's look at differences between someone with a low level of resilience compared to someone with a higher level of resilience.

Again, if you are a person that gives up when things get tough, a person who makes mistakes and doesn't want to try again, or a person who runs away or gets really upset when things don't go their way, then you are a person who has a lower level of resilience. But, if you are a person who accepts their mistakes and moves forward, a person who tries over and over again, or a person who faces challenges head on instead of shying away from them, then you have a higher level of resilience. You can almost think of resilience as your level of happiness, but there is a slight difference. Both happiness and resilience involve different situations that occur in your life. I've read that happiness depends on your perception of what is happening in your life in a particular moment, whereas joy is eternal and everlasting. The key difference between happiness and resilience is that resilience acknowledges the idea that even though there may be hard times, you can still get up again even when you've been knocked down. You can bounce back and move forward. But not only that, as you continue to move forward, be joyful with your life. In other words, be glad as you overcome obstacles and continue to be a better person despite any hardships that you may endure. Joy is that feeling of being positive no matter what. Resilience in the midst of a hard time can lead to your joy. The amount of time it takes to move past or "get over" something hard can indicate your level of resilience. The longer it takes to "get over" something or to feel happy again, the lower your level of resilience. The faster it takes to "get over" something, the higher your level of resilience. Now, this doesn't mean that you should go through life without ever feeling sad, mad, or upset in any kind of way. People are human. Having emotions is natural and part of being a human. Feeling disappointed when you lose a game or feeling sad when you lose a loved one is what makes you human. Trees have resilience but they do not have emotions like a human (well…that's what I'm assuming, but I've never been a tree before). Strong trees have the ability to weather any kind of weather. Strong trees stay rooted to the ground instead of going indoors when it's too hot outside or too cold outside (that would be a strange sight to see). Strong trees can make it through several storms. Strong trees may shed their leaves during the fall and winter months, but they come back year after year. So, I encourage you to stay strong and rooted like a tree. Stand your ground during the not so good times. But, if you need to walk away (such as when a person says something mean to you and you need to prevent yourself from saying or doing something back that could get you in trouble), like a tree that shed's its leaves and seeds, come back stronger the next time. Be like a strong resilient tree instead of a weak and less resilient flower (they may look pretty, but a strong gust of wind can pluck them up and ruin their day or even their life). As a final example, a person who can withstand being called something mean from someone else and still go about their day as if nothing happened, is far more resilient than a person who gets upset and stays upset as soon as they hear one bad thing about themselves. Oh yeah, did I mention that even if you already have a lot of resilience, you can still take it to the next level. Imagine a tree that never stops growing. As the tree weathers different storms and seasons, it can continue to grow and live, or it can eventually get knocked over and die. People are the same way. We can choose to weather a storm and get through it, or we can let the storm beat us down. There's an old saying: "You are either leaving a storm, in the middle of a storm, or getting ready for a storm." No matter who you are or how much money you have, you will face hardships. No one has a perfect life where every little thing goes their way. We all have different obstacles to overcome and different problems to endure. We all have to be strong enough to face them without turning back. That is the essence of resilience and the key to success. So how can you continue to take your resilience to the next level?

Let's continue to use the analogy of the tree. When you look at a tree, it has several components. There are the roots, branches, leaves, fruits, seeds, and the trunk. The roots of a tree provide a solid foundation. The roots keep the tree stable. In fact, that's why the roots are the first part of the tree that is formed after the seed is planted. Without the roots, the tree would not be able to stay in place nor would it receive the water and nutrients from the soil. A resilient person has roots, too. For people, their roots can be their family, friends, or maybe even their religion.

After you are born, your first interactions are with your family. To take it one step further, before you were born, your parents and ancestors planted the seed that turned into the person that you are today. They provided nutrients and lessons that have helped shape your life and the lives of the people that came before you. They may have introduced you to a religion that has served as a major foundation of your life and how you choose to live it. Shortly after those familial interactions, you met other people and developed friendships. These too played a huge role in shaping your life. All of these interactions helped shape how you see the world and what you think about the world. Those interactions can also help influence your interests and goals. The way that you interact with your family and friends can impact how you handle your career and make the decisions that will continue to impact your life and the people that you come into contact with in your life. For example, the way that you are raised by your parents can help influence how you may raise your children. If your parents raised you with strict rules, you may consider whether or not to raise your children that way. As another example, the way that you show affection and the way that you communicate with your friends (which also could have been influenced by your family interactions) can transfer into how you interact with the people that you work with in your career. For many people with a strong enough faith, their religion serves as the basis for everything in their life including their perceptions of the world, their interactions with other people, and how they choose to live their life.

As I continue with the comparison of a tree to a human in regards to resilience, let's take a look at another level. Again, the tree has roots which serve as the foundation. For humans, the foundation or thing that keeps them grounded, can be their family, friends, and religion. Now the next two parts of the tree that I am going to discuss are the branches and leaves. As the tree grows, its branches reach out and sprout leaves which in turn help the tree support itself. The branches are what the tree uses to support the leaves that it produces. The leaves support the nourishment of the entire tree and any fruits that the tree produces. For humans, the "branches" that reach out can be the skills that the human develops over time and the "leaves" are the product of those skills. I'll explain this analogy with an example. Let's say you have the "branch" or the "skill" of running fast. As you continue to grow with this skill, your "leaves" or "product" can be the races that you win. These wins can in return encourage you to continue growing with this "branch" or "skill." In other words, you may become motivated to run faster and faster and work harder and harder. Much like the branches and leaves on a tree that encourage, motivate, and support the growth of the whole tree, the result of your skills (your wins from running your races) can encourage, motivate, and support your growth in that skill and you as a whole person. But what's the point of having these "branches" and "leaves?"

Without the branches and leaves, the tree would just be a twig sticking out of the ground. That sounds pretty boring doesn't it? Branches and leaves give the tree character. Your skills, whether they be your talents and knowledge, are what gives you character. Not only that, in the case of the tree, the branches and leaves enhances the tree and promotes it growth above ground. What are your branches? What are your skills? What are you using to promote your growth? What are you using to not only stand above ground but to also stand out from other people? No one wants to be a boring a person. Use your skills to produce awesome results which can encourage you to stand up, stand out, and keep growing.

As a tree grows, it can produce fruits and seeds. These fruits and seeds go on to produce the next generation of trees. As you grow, you can produce "seeds," as well. These seeds are the influence that you have over another person's life which can promote their growth. Let me explain this by continuing the example of a person who has the skill of running fast. This person's seed can be how they encourage and teach their friends to run fast. Or, it may be the knowledge that they bestow on a younger person who wants to be a faster runner. Think of a coach training an athlete. The coach is usually someone who is older and has played that sport before. But now, they want to train others (the next generation) in that skill so that those other people will have awesome results. The tree who produces fruits and seeds to help future trees grow is similar to a person who uses their skills and knowledge to help others and produce the "fruits" and "seeds" in other people's lives.

So, we discussed how a tree is similar to a person. The tree has its roots as a foundation. A person can have their family, friends, and religion as their foundation. The tree has branches and leaves that encourage and influence its growth and character. A person develops skills, which in return, produces the results of those skills. A tree has fruit and seeds that lead to the growth of the next generation of trees. A person can interact with another person that can lead to that other person's growth. But there is one last part of the tree that makes everything worthwhile. That part is the trunk.

Within the tree's trunk, you will find its heart. Within a person, you will find their heart. The trunk of the whole tree is similar to the body of the whole person. Behind a person's "roots" (family and friends), "branches" (skills), "leaves" (results of those skills), and "fruits and seeds" (influence on the life of others), you will find the actual person at the core of all of this. The tree uses its roots, branches, and leaves as instruments of resilience to support its core, the trunk. Remember that word resilience? It's about bouncing back and moving forward. It's about staying happy in the midst of hard times. It's about being joyful as you continue to move forward. Resilience, can be seen as your strength to overcome obstacles. The strength of a tree is found in a combination of its roots, trunk, branches, leaves, and even its fruits and seeds. This can be the same for a person, too. What motivates you? What keeps you going? Where does your strength come from? What gives you a sense of growing as a person who has a positive impact on others, your community, and maybe even the whole world? As you focus on what are the "roots, trunk, branches, leaves, fruits, and seeds" that are part of your life, you can use these to consider the strengths that you can use to overcome your hardships and to continue moving forward as person. Again, if you ever get knocked down, use your strengths and resilience to bounce back and move forward. Use your resilience to be happy and joyful no matter what.

Final Words

I encourage you to consider and fill in the following diagram according to how it relates to your life:

Roots (what is my foundation)?

_____

Trunk (who am I)?

_____

Branches (what are my skills)?

_____

Leaves (what am I trying to get with my skills…or what have I already gotten with my skills)?

_____

Fruits and Seeds (what do I do to positively influence others)?

_____

CHAPTER 5

More Precious than Gold

They say that the golden rule is to "treat others the way you would like to be treated." Now, this rule is truly valuable, and it can go a long way. But, I want to take this already valuable golden rule, and make it even more valuable. Did you know that diamonds are worth more than gold? Now, if the golden rule is to "treat others the way you would like to be treated," then the diamond rule is simply to "treat others." Let me explain this further.

You may be wondering, what makes this new rule better than the golden rule. There's nothing at all wrong with the golden rule. Respect goes a long way. People should get along with each other because we share this planet called Earth with each other. Times of war and chaos are the result of people not respecting each other. If you don't want to get hurt by someone else, then you shouldn't be hurting them. This moral value, known as respect, is universal. No matter the person's A-B-C-D's (attitude, beliefs, condition, or demographic), everyone is a person. Because of that, everyone deserves respect. How great would the world be if everyone showed more respect to each other? The diamond rule is a step beyond respect. With the golden rule, you expect others to respect you in return. Again, there's nothing wrong with that. Everyone is equal and should be treated fairly. But, have you ever been in a situation where you were really nice to someone and that other person did not return the favor. Maybe that other person did something mean to you instead. Does this mean you were wrong for being nice to them in the first place? Perhaps you felt some regret, but it doesn't mean you were wrong for being nice to that person. It always shows good character when you are nice to someone else even if they are not nice in return. Don't let someone's attitude towards you interfere with your time to shine as a person with awesome character. Who knows, your shine could brighten that person's day and they can shine, too. Maybe they will keep the chain going and continue to brighten the day of someone else. Not only that, have you ever done something for someone and it just made you feel good. A feeling of warmth may have been felt in your chest area and that same warm feeling may have moved all over your body. That was your heart pumping and your body glowing. Congratulations! You experienced the joy of caring for someone else besides yourself. What if you could experience that same warmth and joy every day? I believe you can because it is in our nature. Drop the end of treat others the way you would like to be treated. Just treat others. Don't always expect something in return, because it may not always be given. Focus on treating others. Have a nature to cater. If you follow the Diamond Rule, you will focus on the simple idea of "treat others."

As humans, we each have hearts and brains. These gifts allow us to have feelings and express our emotions. We are also designed with the ability to not just think of ourselves, but to also think about other people, as well. I believe that our design and purpose as humans is to care for ourselves and each other. I believe when you experience that warm feeling of doing something for someone else, that feeling confirms that you have done something great and it fits what we are supposed to do. When you flip a light switch, it causes the light to illuminate a room. This is the purpose of the switch. Like that light switch, when you care about someone else, it causes you to feel amazing. This is part of your purpose. So, go out and be altruistic, care for others, feel proud, and live an extraordinary life. I hope that you can rise above the Golden Rule and move towards the Diamond Rule. But wait, there's one rule that's even more valuable than the Diamond Rule.

What's more valuable than a diamond? Well, if you do the research, there are many things that are more expensive than a diamond such as painite, californium, and even a substance known as antimatter. What makes these items so valuable is their rarity. A substance's value can be based on how much of that substance you can find in nature. Things that are easy to find in nature due to their abundance may cost less than something that is hard to find in nature because there is so little of it. However, did you know that you are the only you in the world? Did you know that no two people are exactly alike? Even identical twins are different from each other. How is it that in a world of billions and billions of people, no two people are exactly alike? Each person has their own unique physical experience that is hard to replicate. You can search for your entire lifetime and you will never find someone that has your same height, eye color, hair color, hair length, nose, ears, shade of skin, blood type, fingerprints, or DNA all in exactly the same combination as what makes up you. Not only that, we all come to the table with different experiences and perceptions. No one has lived the exact same life as you. Who else grew up with your parents as their parents, your siblings as their siblings, living at your address, sleeping in your bed, wearing your clothes, walking around in your body, thinking your thoughts, and seeing the world through your eyes. NO ONE! And if you really think about it, you are also different from your reflection in the mirror. How is that so? Think about it. Your reflection may see what you see, but it sees everything that you see…in reverse. That's crazy when you really think about it. If you look in the mirror and wink your left eye, it looks like your reflection is winking its right eye. I'm not trying to blow your mind, but I am trying to make a point. No one sees the world exactly like you do. Even your reflection has a different perception. Two people may perceive something as simple as a blue crayon differently. Not only will they have different past experiences with blue crayons, but they may actually physically see the same crayon differently. The way that their eyes see the same blue crayon may be different from each other. One person may see one shade while the other person sees another shade that could be extremely similar but slightly different. Why is that? Those two people do not have the same eyes nor the same brain. So because of the differences in our experiences and perceptions, each individual person is the rarest substance in the world because each individual person is the only version of that individual person in existence. Due to the rarity of each individual's unique life, we can conclude that each person's life is far more valuable than anything else that you will find in the universe. You have a better chance of finding even more of the other rare matters in the universe than finding two people that are EXACTLY alike. Remember that antimatter stuff that I mentioned earlier. It is one of the rarest substances found in the universe. There is a little more than one gram of it. But, you are the only you in existence, and the same goes for everyone else. Now, because that goes for everyone, shouldn't we treat everyone as if they are extremely precious and valuable?

So, what's more valuable than a diamond? Well, I think I pointed out the most valuable thing in the world. Human life is something that we can't really place a value on. It is something that is so valuable that it is invaluable. I've pointed out this fact for a reason. First, we took a look at the Golden Rule. Then, we took a look at the Diamond Rule because it is more valuable than the Golden Rule. The last rule that I would like to discuss is a rule that is more valuable and precious than the last two. I would like to call it the Life Rule.

What is the Life Rule? Well, it is actually only one step further than the Diamond Rule, but it can go a long way. The Life Rule is to treat others BETTER than you would like to be treated. Before I explain this rule, keep in mind that everyone is equal and no one is better or lesser than anyone else. The Life Rule doesn't imply that you treat anyone like they are better than you or as if you are lesser than them. Sometimes when we treat other people, we may expect something in return. We may expect respect or we may expect something as small as a thank you. This is the Golden Rule. Sometimes we may not expect anything, but we just want to be nice to someone. This is the Diamond Rule. You may be wondering, what could be better than doing something just to be nice to someone. Let me give a few examples. Have you ever heard about celebrities donating money to build schools or giving donations to different charities? These celebrities are following the Life Rule. They are doing something more than just an act to be nice to someone. They are doing something that can make a difference in someone's life for the better. They are helping to build schools so that children can obtain an education. One of those children may eventually grow up, become a doctor, and may even find the cure for cancer. These celebrities are helping to provide playgrounds or different recreation activities and centers for children who may not have been exposed to them otherwise. One of those children may be from a violent, poor, and disadvantaged area. But, because they now have a safe place to play and learn instead of becoming a member of a gang, they could grow up to become the mayor of that same city and make it a safer and more productive place for the children that would come later. In these two examples, these celebrities may have the money to help them achieve these projects. Still, it's not the money that makes the difference. Money can be one of the stepping stones. Regardless, of whether money is involved or not, the difference is made when you do something to help someone else along the way. These celebrities could be spending their money on many other things, but instead, they are using it to help other people. And not only that, in these two examples, the people that are helped are the ones that can grow up and make a huge difference in the lives of more and more people. It's like a ripple effect. One drop ripples and spreads beyond the center and reaches places far beyond where it began. Similarly, one special act can spread beyond one person and can even spread on for generations. Two people come to mind when I think of the Life Rule. One person is Rev. Dr. Martin Luther King Jr. He put other people before him, stood up for civil rights, and started a change that would extend for generations. The other person that comes to mind is Jesus Christ, the author and finisher of the Christian faith. Not only did he teach people how to treat others, he also saved the entire world and provided an amazing grace that would extend for generation after generation of Christian believers. Both of these people died doing things that would benefit other people. They both achieved fame not because of their deaths, but because of what they accomplished.

The Life Rule is more than doing a kind act without expecting something in return. It is about treating someone better than they may treat you. It is about doing something for someone who may not be able to do the same for you. When celebrities donate money to help feed the poor, they are not expecting money or food in return. So, why do it? Yes, it is the right thing to do. But what makes it the right thing? I believe we have a duty to look after each other. I believe love is the greater than anything we can possess or give. Through love, we can truly understand what it means to do something for someone without expecting anything in return. Through love we can really start to help someone for the right reason. Acts of love are better than acts of kindness. It is easy to show an act of kindness. But showing an act of love is something that takes more effort. Here's an example. Let's say you know someone who may be unpopular. Maybe this person doesn't have anyone that they can talk to you because they don't have any friends. An act of kindness towards this person would be to say hi to them the next time you see them. An act of love would be to have a conversation with this person and become friends with them. Love is more than a simple act. Love is showing that you care about someone. Love goes a long way. Love is the greatest. With so many people in the world, wouldn't it be amazing if we all loved each other. There may be times where people may not agree with each other or mistakes may be made, but with love, anything can be overcome. With more love in the world, not only would there be less violence and less hate, there would be more working together. With more love in the world, people would realize that we are all more alike than different. We all have hopes, wants, and needs. Joy and happiness are two precious things that everyone searches for and hopes to possess. Wouldn't the world be a better place if we helped each other obtain that joy and happiness? We all have beating hearts and thinking brains. We should all use them for the benefit of ourselves and for each other.

So, how can all of this apply to you? Well, you can be a celebrity in someone's life. Do something for them not so they can remember you, but to make a difference in their life. Spread love to others and hopefully they will keep that chain of love going. Think about the examples that I gave earlier with the celebrities helping to build schools and the celebrities helping to build recreation activities and centers. You don't have to spend money to make a difference in the life of another person. You can spend your time visiting some of the elderly people in your community. Show them that someone cares about them and listen to what they have to say (you might learn something). You can also be on the lookout for those people that are just in the need of a friend or someone to talk to who cares about them. This is another example I gave earlier. I am giving it again because there are so many people in the world who can benefit and have benefitted from just talking to someone who cares. Here's another example that may be hard to wrap your head around at first. Befriend a bully. Many times a person who bullies others is actually crying out for help. They may be crying for help in the wrong way, but does that mean they need less help? Showing love and care towards a bully can not only help them realize the error of their ways, it can also help them heal from whatever caused them to resort to bullying in the first place. Not to mention, it can help the people that they used to bully especially if the bully stops the bullying behavior.

Here's something else for you to think about…you can encourage other people to follow the Life Rule. I really hope that you have seen that the Life Rule is more precious than both the Golden Rule as well as the Diamond Rule. Your acts of love can go a long way because when you put other people before yourself and help them, it can make a huge difference not only in their life, but also in the lives that they can come in contact with, too. Now when you encourage other people to follow the Life Rule, and all of you follow it fully, it can create a huge positive effect. Many huge changes in the world started with one person who had an idea. Not only that, that person believed in that idea so much that they stood for it and encouraged others to do the same. Does your community need something? Maybe it could use a little more love. What can you do about it? Be the ripple of change that can have a tidal wave effect. With the help of other like-minded people, you can cause a world of difference for your community. Your actions could possibly reach beyond your community. Think about Martin Luther King Jr. or even Jesus Christ. No, I'm not saying that you have to put your life on the line and possibly die for your idea. I'm a Professional School Counselor and of course I want everyone to be safe. However, I am saying to stand up for your idea especially if it is something that can benefit you and other people. Don't worry about each discouragement. Instead, seek to be an encouragement as you lift up others who may have a hard time lifting themselves up. Remember not to expect anything in return because sometimes people don't have the resources, time, or whatever else to reciprocate something that you give them or do for them. Maybe they are still learning how to show love and you can be their teacher. Do unto others better than they can do unto you. You are no better than anyone else. No one else is better than you. But, you can put others before you. You can be that special agent of change that someone else needs to achieve their greatness. Remember that warm feeling in your chest that I spoke about earlier with the Diamond Rule? Well, with the Life Rule, you will feel like you are on fire. Be thankful for each and every experience that you will encounter whether they are good or bad. Stay strong and use each experience as a lesson to develop your greater self. With everything you learn, use it along with the Life Rule to help benefit those around you. Even though you may not be doing it for the fame or celebrity status, you may always be remembered by someone that you sincerely loved and helped. Life is the most valuable substance in the entire universe. When we treat it as such, we start to understand what it means to love and how to love. In return, love causes life to be better in more and more ways especially if there are more and more people involved. For all of these reasons, the Life Rule is more precious than gold.

Final Words

Golden Rule: Treat others the way you would like to be treated

(RESPECT)

Diamond Rule: Treat others

(ALTRUISM)

Life Rule: Treat others better than you would like to be treated

(HUMILITY)

CHAPTER 6

Making the GRADE

Goals, Restrictions, Actions, Decisions, and Evaluations

Now we come to the chapter where the book gets its name. Making the Grade does not imply making a good grade on a test or school assignment. Instead, it focuses more on accomplishing goals for yourself and continuing to better your life. GRADE is actually an acronym for you to keep in mind as you consider, work towards, and achieve your goals. So, without further ado, let's get started with that first letter, G.

G stands for Goals. Sounds simple enough doesn't it? That's why this is the perfect place to start. Plus, it works out having G as the beginning letter in the word GRADE. Another reason why this is the perfect place to start, is because many people do not take the time to consider an actual, well-thought out goal.

As a Professional School Counselor, I often teach my students about SMART goals. If you guessed that SMART is another acronym…you guessed right! SMART stands for Specific, Measurable, Achievable, Relevant, and Timely. I often hear goals such as "I want to get better at math," "I want to be a good basketball player," or "I want to get faster at running." All of these goals sound like excellent things to shoot for, but they always leave me with the same question…WHAT DO YOU MEAN BY THAT? If someone hears about your goal and they don't really know what you are talking about, then that means your goal is not specific enough. The purpose of having a Specific goal is to give you a strong sense of direction towards your goal. In other words, with a Specific goal, you will know exactly what you are trying to achieve. Now, let's talk about one of the non-specific goals that I mentioned earlier. What does getting better at math mean? Is there a particular area in math that you want to focus on? Do you need help with all math skills such as knowing how to count from one to ten? Instead of keeping a non-specific goal, give yourself direction by making it specific. Instead of setting a non-specific goal such as "I want to get better at math," you could set a specific goal such as "I want to be able to recite the twelve times multiplication table from one to ten in less than ten seconds," or "I want to make at least an 85% on my next math test about multiplication." The more specific the goal, the better you can set your sights on shooting for it. Let's take a look at the next letter, M.

When your goal is Measurable, you can monitor your progress towards achieving it. For example, if you want to run a mile in six minutes, you may practice running the mile multiple times. Your first attempt may result in a time of seven minutes. Your next attempt may result in a time six minutes and thirty seconds. Your third attempt may result in a time of six minutes and fifteen seconds. If you look at these times, you can see that you are moving closer and closer to your goal. This progress shows that you are doing something to make your goal more and more reachable. Maybe you start stretching more and more to get your body more prepared to run. Maybe you changed up your diet. The purpose of looking at the results as you work on your goal is to make sure you are moving in the right direction. But what if the situation was reversed. What if you had the same goal of wanting to run a mile in six minutes, but on the first attempt, you ran the mile in seven minutes. On the next attempt, you ran the mile in seven minutes and fifteen seconds. On the third attempt, you ran the mile in seven minutes and twenty seconds. Looking at these results, you can see that you are moving farther and farther away from your goal. There could be something that you are doing to make your goal harder to achieve. Maybe you are eating a heavy meal before you run or maybe you are not getting enough sleep or maybe you aren't stretching before you run.

Don't worry, we'll get to the rest of the letters in our GRADE acronym. But, let's finish up our SMART acronym first. So, the next letter is A. Is your goal Achievable? In other words, is it possible to accomplish your goal? You shouldn't set a goal that is impossible. No one should set a goal to flap their arms fast enough to fly. Although it would be amazing to see, it is still impossible. Setting an impossible goal is just a set up for failure. Now even though you shouldn't set an impossible goal, you also shouldn't set a goal that is too easy to achieve. For example, what is the point of setting a goal of doing five push-ups in a minute if you can easily do twenty in a minute? Sure, you may feel a small amount of accomplishment, but you really didn't have to work that hard to accomplish that easy goal. Whenever you set a goal, you should set a goal that is going to require work. If you push yourself to achieve a hard goal, then you will obtain more satisfaction after you achieve that hard goal compared to achieving an easy goal. I don't know about you, but after I accomplish a goal, I would rather say "Yes, I did it" instead of "Umm…now what." Goals are more meaningful if they are more than just something to accomplish.

Setting and working towards goals should also make you a better person in the process. This leads to the R in SMART. What makes your goal Relevant? Why is setting a particular goal important to you? Why do you want to be able to bench press two hundred pounds? Maybe you want to work towards being a physically stronger person. Why do you want to be able to make ten free throws in a row? Maybe you want be a better free throw shooter so that your basketball team can rely on you to make the shot. When you set a goal that is important to you, it becomes more than a goal. It becomes a mission. You will be more dedicated to see it through if it is important to you.

The T in SMART stands for Timely. When you set a goal, it is beneficial to have a time frame to complete it. This time frame gives your goal more meaning because you have a sense of finishing it in a certain time instead of aimlessly working at it until you eventually get it done. For some people, they may never get it done unless they have a time to get it done. Some people have the mindset of "I'll work on it later." But, later never gets here. If you keep putting something off, when will you ever work on it. When you set your goal, set a time frame along with it. When are you trying to accomplish your goal? Did you set time to take breaks so that you don't overwork yourself and stress yourself out? When you become overly stressed, it makes the process even harder and less enjoyable. Consider all of this when you set your timely goal.

Don't you want your goal to be SMART? Who wants a dumb goal? If you want to make your goal SMART, it has to be Specific, Measureable, Achievable, Relevant, and Timely. Success comes from smart thinking, good decisions, and hard work. So, why not set SMART goals to help you along the way.

Okay, so let's get back to the title of this book and this chapter. GRADE is what it's all about. I've spent quite a bit of time talking about the G, which stands for Goal. Now it's time to talk about the next four letters. R stands for Restrictions. In other words, what are the things that can keep you from moving forward? While walking this earth, I believe three things can happen...you can move backwards, stay in place, or you can move forward. What if you had the time to really think about your SMART goal, but there is still something that is holding you back? After all, if you aren't moving forward, then there has to be a reason. For some people, they take the Good Enough Approach. They are satisfied with "just getting by" instead of putting forth their absolute best effort. They can make an A on a graded assignment, but they would rather settle on making a C because that's good enough. Unfortunately, what they fail to realize is that growth, strength, and success comes from being tested and overcoming stress. A common piece of carbon can become a precious diamond if it goes through the proper process with the right amount of heat and pressure. A successful person has to go through a similar process. An ordinary person can become a big success if they are not only exposed to the proper conditions, but if they overcome those conditions, as well. If you take a look at many of the celebrities of today, you will see that many of them, like Oprah Winfrey, grew up in humble and sometimes below humble conditions. Poverty, medical conditions, and harsh relationships are some examples of stressful restrictions. Restrictions are those things that can hold you back, or, they can make you stronger. For the people that go beyond the Good Enough Approach, strength is something that is gained along the way. Strength comes from grit. Grit comes from persistence and resilience. Persistence simply means to never give up. Resilience simply means bounce back, move forward...sound familiar? Grit means you have an attitude of altitude. It's believing that nothing can hold you back and that you will continue to move forward and climb higher and higher. Instead of settling for the Good Enough Approach, a successful person will get gritty and have the What's Next Approach. Will you have restrictions in your life? Of course you will. Everyone faces restrictions and setbacks. No one has a perfect life where everything goes their way all of the time. However, setbacks are opportunities to rise up and flex your strengths. There's a difference between life and living. When you are faced with obstacles and burdens that way you down, that's life. When you step over obstacles and carry yourself to higher places, that's living.

The biggest restriction is yourself. I know that may sound a little strange. Think of it this way. You are your biggest critic. You have a choice in everything you say, do, and believe. Whether someone gives you a compliment or an insult, you can choose to believe them or not. You can always walk away from other people, but you have to live with yourself no matter what. At the beginning and end of the day, you have the first and final say. Our thoughts come from what we say to ourselves. Our thoughts lead to our actions. The letter A in our GRADE acronym stands for Actions. What are you doing with your life? What are you going to do with your life? What do you need to do to achieve success? Take action. Fill your head with positive thoughts so that you can build yourself up and pursue positive actions. Some people restrict themselves and put themselves down with negative thoughts. They may think about what they can't do, or they may have a bad attitude about themselves. Other people raise themselves up with positive thoughts. They think about what they can do or what they will become able to do. These are the kind of people who have a good attitude about themselves because they love themselves and believe in themselves. I believe life is 40% what you think internally and 40% what you do externally. Stick around for the last 20%. Your actions, which are found on the outside, are a reflection of your thoughts, which are found on the inside. In other words, what you do tends to go along with what you think. If you think you can do something, your actions will prove it. If you don't think you can do something, then your actions will prove that, as well. People who "fail" are the ones who think about giving up and actually give up. People who are successful think about being successful even in the midst of a not so pleasant time. Still, success doesn't just come from thinking about it. Most people want to be successful, but only a few put in the work to actually do it. Take action and work hard. That means that you have to be willing to dedicate the time, energy, and everything you can muster to make it happen. You have to put EVERYTHING you got into doing what you need to do.

We are almost at the end of the GRADE acronym. The next letter, D, stands for Decisions. Before I go into detail about the Decisions aspect of the GRADE acronym, let me remind you of the G. In the Goals process, time is spent creating a plan about a specific goal and how to come closer to achieving it. The D, or Decisions, process is geared towards choices that can cause you to continue or discontinue your goal. No matter what goal you may set for yourself, you will have restrictions that can get in the way of accomplishing your goal. We've talked about this before with the R. With every restriction, you can make a decision to continue or discontinue trying to accomplish your goal. Maybe after taking a look at the possible restrictions, you plan and start the actions to accomplish your goal, but it still seems like your goal is too hard to reach. Again, goals should be set that are hard to achieve so that you can gain more satisfaction after achieving them. But, you may have to make a decision to alter your goal. There is nothing wrong with altering your goal. People change their minds all of the time. I originally went to The College of William and Mary to become a lawyer because I wanted to help people. But, I altered my goal to become a Professional School Counselor because I thought about helping people at a young age. Even if you make the decision to alter your goal, you can still move forward towards success. You just have to make the decision to move forward instead of sitting still, moving backwards, or quitting completely. Besides making the decision to move forward, you may also have to make the decision to move some things to the side. Remember that it's a good idea to take breaks, but don't let your breaks overshadow your goals. Restrictions can come in the form of people who can draw you away from accomplishing your goal. It may be innocent. You may find yourself in situations where you can decide to work on your goal or hang out with your friends. Both are good ideas, but if you really want to accomplish something, you're going to have to put in some work sometime. Also, never ever serve as your own restriction. Don't let laziness or a bad attitude get in your way. Don't forget to flex your strengths, bounce back, and move forward.

Remember when I said life is 40% what you think internally and 40% what you do externally? The other 20% comes with the last letter in the GRADE acronym. The letter E stands for Evaluation. Whether you set a goal for yourself or not, you should always take the time to evaluate yourself and how your life is going. Are you happy with the current status of your life? Are you happy with yourself as a person? These are two basic questions that may have some not so basic answers if you put some serious thought into them. Hmm…sounds similar to the reflections that I spoke about earlier! People often have heart to hearts with each other, but there should be times where you should have an honest heart to heart with yourself. An evaluation like this can cause major life decisions. I believe that people should always want better for themselves. Still, a person's life doesn't tend to get better unless they truly want it for themselves. Everyone has that friend with problems that seem so easy to fix. "All they have to do is…" We may know the answer, but it's not our life or our decision to make for them. Until they realize the answer and put in the work to fix the problem, things may stay the same or become worse. Maybe they need to evaluate their life with those two basic questions. Are you happy with the current status of your life? Are you happy with yourself as a person? Here's another thought for you...it may be easy figure out the answer to another person's problem. Sometimes it's easier being on the outside looking in. But, what if the roles were reversed? You may find yourself in the middle of a problem and your friend may have figured out the answer. Hmmm…not so fun is it! Again, sometimes it's easier being on the outside looking in. Either way, it pays to have that heart to heart. You may have a heart to heart with someone else about an issue they are facing, but at the end of the day, it's still their decision to make because it is their life to live. Likewise, if someone has a heart to heart with you, it is still your decision to make afterwards. Evaluate yourself, your life, and your goals. If you are happy with how things are going, then continue doing what you are doing. If you are getting closer to accomplishing your goal and you are still happy with the goal that you have set for yourself, then continue along that same path. This means that you have developed a SMART Goal that you are happy with, you feel happy and confident about overcoming any of the Restrictions that can get in your way, you are happy with your Actions, and your Decisions are causing you to experience happiness, too. Still, I believe there is a third basic question to help you evaluate your life so that you can experience absolute and everlasting joy beyond momentary happiness:

1. Are you happy with the current status of your life?
2. Are you happy with yourself as a person?
3. What would make things better?

Final Words

I believe life is a constant evolution to reach your full potential. There is always room for growth even after you achieve success. There should always be goals to accomplish and ways to make yourself a better person. We may never achieve perfection, but we can always work towards it. I believe you should never settle for less than your best, and if you can always do better, then your best is yet to come. Life is 40% what you think internally, 40% what you do externally, and 20% how you evaluate it.

CHAPTER 7

Me, Myself, I, and You

I bet you have been waiting for this chapter. This book would not be complete without a chapter on relationships. For most people, after they reach a certain age of maturity, relationships is a subject that becomes a huge focus. For some people, relationships is all they think and talk about. Now I bet when I say relationship, you may think that I am talking about something between you and another person. Although that is true, one of the most important relationships that you will ever have in your life, is your relationship with yourself.

Before you love anyone else or even think about falling in love with someone else, you have to love yourself. You have to get to know yourself before you let someone else get to know you. Be an expert on all things about you. In chapter one, I mentioned that you only know yourself on the surface level. After you do some reflections and spend the time to get to know yourself on a deeper level, you will start to understand what makes you tick, what you are really into, and what makes you...you. It takes some people years to understand what they are really about because they learn through trial and error. Have you ever gone into something thinking that you would enjoy it, but it turns out that you really hated it? Maybe you thought that you would really like baseball, softball, playing the piano, or something else that you thought you would be into, but it turned out to not be the case at all? Yes, you may not know what you like until you try it. Still, take the time to try it and get to know yourself. As you get older, you may find the same trial and error pattern with your future career. Or, maybe you are already experiencing that perfect career search right now. Either way, take your time and reflect on yourself and your experiences. Think about what you enjoy and what brings you the most joy. After all, isn't that how you want to live your life? I believe you should be able to live happily with yourself before you can let someone else into your life. Why is it important to have a relationship with yourself before you have a relationship with someone else? Well, after you get to know you, you can find someone who is the perfect complement to you. They say that opposites attract. That's true for magnets, but you are not a magnet. Sometimes people who are the polar opposite of each other can make things work for their relationship. But in my experience and from what I have seen from others, those relationships where people share more similarities than differences are the relationships that are stronger and last longer. Before you look for a relationship, take the time to understand your values. In other words, what is important to you? I've done an exercise where I not only listed my values, I also wrote why those values were important to me and what I was looking for in someone else. Do you value religion, honesty, family, and communication? Why? What else is important to you? After you understand what is important to you and the reason behind what makes it important, you can have a good idea of what you are looking for in another person.

Creating a list of your values can give you more insight on finding what you are actually looking for instead of getting distracted along the way. Use your list of values as a map that will help you get to your destination, which could be the arms of the person of your dreams. Similarly, use your list of values as a list of ingredients for your love muffin recipe. Hahaha I hope you liked that one. Either way, taking the time to create a list of values and reflect on those values can benefit you in the long run. When you have a better idea of what you are looking for, you are more likely to find it. If you find someone who has the same values as you, it will feel like a match made in heaven. Enjoy your trip for two to paradise!

Many times, people will want to rush into a relationship and lose sight on what is actually best for themselves. I've known people who will chase after someone they thought they loved, and in the process, they lost themselves. They became a different person, and I'm not talking about in a good way. You may know someone like this. I've known people who had a bright future in front of themselves and then all of that changed for the worse because they wanted to pursue a relationship with someone that turned their dream of a happy future into a nightmare. You may know someone like this, too. Hopefully, you will not find yourself in this kind of situation. I've known people who weren't happy with their life and they believed that if they found someone, then that would make their life better. Instead, they found out that their life became worse. If you have some problems in your life, do not expect that someone can fix those problems. Why? If you expect that someone else will fix those problems but they don't fix those problems, you may continue to have those same problems along with a new problem on top of them. That person that you thought was going to fix those problems may turn into a disappointment. That person may even take your focus away from fixing your own problems. Now if you have problems, and someone else has problems, all of these problems could possibly lead to chaos. Nobody's life is perfect or will ever be perfect, but when it comes to a relationship with someone else, shouldn't it be as best as it could be especially at the start?

Final Words

Your life should be the cake and your partner is the icing on the cake. No matter what kind of cake you have, you need the proper ingredients and steps to make sure it comes out right. Work on building yourself first. When you make a cake, you don't add the icing to the eggs, flour, and the other ingredients to make the cake. Again, fix your ingredients first and follow the proper steps. What do you need for yourself and to do for yourself before you bring in someone else? Wait until you (the cake) are ready to add someone else in your life (the icing). Even a baked cake needs time to cool down before the icing is added to it.

CHAPTER 8

Living above the Clouds

Have you ever had a really good day? You know, one of those days where it seemed like you were lucky and a lot of things went your way. How did you feel? I bet you felt more than happy. You probably felt amazing and unstoppable. Nothing could ruin that day for you. If you haven't had one of those days yet, keep living and keep reading this book. I am going to tell you the key to having a day like this, and it can happen day after day after day. The key is to live above the clouds.

Even though we walk on the ground, we can live above the clouds. Now, what does that mean? Well, it doesn't mean that your house should be hovering above the clouds. We don't have that kind of technology yet, but maybe someday it will happen. Living above the clouds doesn't mean you should become an airhead. That's somebody who is always dreaming and never really accomplishing anything because they don't focus or work hard. Living above the clouds means to stay positive.

Staying positive can be easy especially if everything is going well. When your happenings are happy, I'm sure you will be, too. In other words when something is going your way and you are surrounded by happy people, it will rub off on you, too. Life can be full of those moments, so take advantage of them especially if you can share them with other people. Those are the moments that make happy memories. Not only should you look forward to those moments, you should also find ways to make those moments happen. If you use the same concepts from our GRADE acronym (Goals, Restrictions, Actions, Decisions, and Evaluations), you can help create your own happiness. Surround yourself with people that can motivate you and lift you up. Make good and wise decisions. Work hard and enjoy your rewards. Trust me, all of this really does pay off. If you focus on creating your happiness, you won't have time to be disappointed.

Now, staying positive also has a lot to do with your mindset. What is a mindset? Simply put, a mindset is how you view events and situations. For example, a person with a negative mindset is quick to point out what's wrong in a situation or what's not to their liking. Sometimes, they even do this when things are not so bad. You may know someone in your life who seems to be upset a lot even over small things. On the other hand, a person with a positive mindset can find the good even in tough situations. They find the silver lining in the storm cloud. They may say something such as, "Even though I didn't make the team, I can still watch the games, work on my skills, and I can try to make the team next time." If you look at these two types of people, it may be obvious that the person with a positive mindset will stay happy more often than the person with a negative mindset. It may also be obvious that the person with a negative mindset will more likely add stress to their life compared to the person with a positive mindset. Remember, life is 40% what you think internally, 40% what you do externally, and 20% how you evaluate it. That last 20% is your mindset. Do you have a positive mindset or a negative mindset? Whether you have the first or the second, I would like to teach you an important concept that can help you stay positive and motivated especially if you are trying to achieve a hard goal. That concept is the "Power of Yet."

Everyone has experienced some sort of failure in their life. In the game of baseball, the batter may strikeout at the plate. In the classroom, the student may not do well on a test. Does this mean these people should give up and never try again? Of course not! Hopefully they will muster up their resilience, bounce back, and move forward. This is when the "Power of Yet" comes into play, as well. There are times when you may not get something right the first time. Everyone has experienced that multiple times in their life. Take a look at a toddler that is trying to walk for the first time. They stumble and fall at first, and that's because they haven't learned how to walk...yet. Sure, they may experience some frustrations just like adults experience frustrations while facing a difficult task. But eventually, if that toddler keeps trying, they will walk and eventually run. The "Power of Yet" comes into play when we tell ourselves "I haven't achieved this...yet." In other words, when we don't understand something the first time or if we fail to do something right the first time, we accept the fact that we are still learning how to accomplish that task and we will accomplish that task eventually. Every success story has a little bit of failure. However, don't let that failure turn into the main story that causes the event of giving up and never moving forward. That's not a happy ending. Acknowledge the failure, evaluate what went wrong, and encourage yourself to fix it. Keep in mind that greatness is not achieved over night. Some of the greatest inventions and discoveries in the world took time to make possible (electricity, lightbulbs, cars, and the list goes on and on). During those times of frustration, don't give up. You may be closer than you think when it comes to accomplishing that goal. Sometimes a small mistake can seem like a big setback. For example, when it comes to big math problems that require multiple steps, a small mistake can cause the entire answer to be wrong. But if you take the time to go through everything step by step and evaluate what led up to the final result, you can find what needed to be fixed. This concept can be used in many aspects of your life especially when it comes to achieving a goal that requires multiple steps along the way. Remember when things get hard or something may be hard to understand, tell yourself that you just haven't achieved it yet, but you will. Keep trying, Make the Grade, and make it happen. A person with a negative mindset will give up more often than trying again, but a person with a positive mindset will rely on the "Power of Yet."

Now, in the midst of frustrations, it is important to relieve stress. Even people with a positive mindset can have some stress in their life during hard situations. Stress can weigh you down especially if you already feel down. That is why I would also like to teach you two ways to relieve stress so that you can refocus on staying positive. The first way is something that I like to call the Find My Breath Game.

The Find My Breath Game is pretty simple. Many times when we are focusing on something that is stressful, it can lead to even more stress. Taking a mental break from the stressor (whatever is causing you stress) until you are ready to tackle it can be a good way to overcome it. When I say take a mental break, I am referring to thinking about something else so that you can calm yourself down, refocus, and become better able to accomplish whatever was stressing you in the first place. Many times when people are stressed, their bodies will display the stress in different ways. Some ways can be headaches, sweating, hard time thinking, feeling sick, and loss of energy. If you want to accomplish something, it is better to get your body calm and ready first. The Find My Breath Game can help take your mind off of what was stressing you so that you can calm your body down. To play the game, you can take a comfortable sitting position. If you are in a room with a chair, feel free to sit in the chair. Next, close your eyes and take two deep breaths. With every deep breath imagine your stomach is a balloon. Try to inflate and deflate your stomach by breathing in deeply through your nose and out through your mouth. I like to call these balloon breaths. You should feel your stomach growing and shrinking. While you are taking your breaths, think of something to look for in the space that you are occupying. Perhaps you can look for a certain color or shape. Once you have decided what you would like to look for, open your eyes and find something that matches what you were trying to find. After you find the object, close your eyes, take two more deep balloon breaths, think of something else to find, and find your new object. This cycle can repeat as many times as necessary. Your goal is to take a break from whatever was stressing you. This does not mean that you are avoiding it completely without ever returning to it again. Instead, you are trying to calm down first so that you can better be able to overcome that stressor. Take a look at my example of a ten round cycle of the Find My Breath Game:

1. Take two deep breaths and then find something red.
2. Take two deep breaths and then find something yellow.
3. Take two deep breaths and then find something green.
4. Take two deep breaths and then find something blue.
5. Take two deep breaths and then find a circle.
6. Take two deep breaths and then find a square.
7. Take two deep breaths and then find a rectangle.
8. Take two deep breaths and then find a triangle.
9. Take two deep breaths and then find something white.
10. Take two deep breaths and then find something black.

While playing this game, remember to close your eyes and take your two balloon breaths at the start of each round. I prefer to play ten rounds, but feel free to play as many as you need to feel calm and ready to overcome your stress. Besides the Find My Breath Game, the other way to relieve stress is another game. It is called the Great Game.

Sometimes when we feel stress, not only can it weigh us down, it can also make it hard to see the great things that are already in our lives. We can forget the things that we are grateful to have in our lives. Playing the Great Game will bring those great things back to the forefront of our minds and we can start to feel better especially if a stressor didn't make us feel so great. The Great Game is another simple game to play. Think of your mind as a basket and you are trying to fill it full of great things. To do that, think of at least five things that you are grateful for. In other words, think of the things that make you happy and proud to have in your life. As you think of something, put it in a sentence beginning with, "It is great to have…" As you complete your sentence, take some time to focus on each great thing that comes to mind. Think about why you are grateful to have that great in your life and maybe even how it came to be in your life. When you take the time to do this, you will feel a sense of happiness and renewed strength. When we take the time to acknowledge the great things in our life, it makes everything brighter. Here are some examples of my greats that I came up with while playing the Great Game:

1. It is great to have God in my life.
2. It is great to have supportive family members and friends in my life.
3. It is great to have love for myself in my life.
4. It is great to have motivation towards my goals in my life.
5. It is great to have my talents and gifts in my life.

The Great Game is an awesome way to stay positive throughout the day. You can play it even if you aren't feeling stressed or upset about something. You can also use it in combination with the Find My Breath Game if something is really bothering. I've played both of these games to help my students calm down, refocus, and reenergize themselves after facing a challenge in their lives. As a Professional School Counselor, I've learned that these kinds of games can really help someone that is facing a hardship. Playing the Find My Breath Game can help bring a sense of calmness to someone who may be feeling sad, angry, or frustrated. After that sense of calmness is regained, playing the Great Game, can bring not only happiness back to their life, but it can also bring a sense of pride, motivation, and empowerment, as well.

Even in the midst of failures and stressors, it is important to acknowledge the things that are already great in your life. By remaining positive, you can give yourself the necessary boost to keep moving forward in the direction of your dreams and goals. Sure, you may feel like your life can be a whole lot better. That in itself may be true. But again, it is beneficial to acknowledge what you already have in your life. I encourage you to encourage yourself. Remember that hard goals may not be achieved instantly. Time may be needed to make your dream a reality. No matter how long it may take, you can have a great time by remaining positive along the way.

Final Words

Living above the clouds can help you elevate yourself to higher places. Staying positive is a key to a long and happy life. Stress does damage to your body and can even shorten your lifespan. But remaining positive can not only strengthen and reenergize your body, it can also help you enjoy your life. Make amazing memories. Take some time to reflect on the great things in your life. Take your time, don't hurry, and be happy.

CHAPTER 9

What's the Next Chapter in Your Life?

The next chapter of this book is dedicated to your future success. Because your future is left up to you, it is now your turn to write the next chapter. Thank you for taking the time to allow me to share some thoughts with you. My purpose behind this book was to plant some seeds of advice in hopes to encourage and assist you to reach your maximum potential. I hope that I have accomplished this purpose. Still, you may have questions that I may not have answered. To those questions, I say…LIVE YOUR LIFE!

Experience is always the best teacher. Whether you speak to someone and hear about their experiences, or go through something yourself, you can always learn something from Experience. You can learn so much from talking to someone who has already been through something. Talk to your elders, talk to professionals, talk to people who love what they do. And after you have grown through your own experiences, share what you have learned with other people. Even as a teacher, you will see that there is still more room for you to grow. Many times, the teacher will learn a lesson along the way. In my life, I have learned so much while serving, helping, mentoring, and counseling others. Do your best to learn, grow, teach, and grow some more. Life presents continual opportunities to transition to a higher position.

As you live your life, remember to remain positive along the way. Overcome those restrictions and keep joy in your life. Develop your goals and flex your strengths. Right now, you are powerful, but overtime, you will become powerful beyond belief. Like a tree that never ceases to stop growing, if you remain resilient, you can reach heights that you didn't think were possible. Remember your roots, stretch your branches, shape your leaves, build up your trunk, and pass along some fruits and seeds along your path of success. Acknowledge your beauty and the beauty in the world around you. Treat yourself and everyone else with the upmost respect and reverence. Be humble and thankful for everything and everyone. Make good decisions and let your positive thoughts influence your positive actions. Get to know yourself better as you become a better person. Take the time to have those moments of reflection, because evaluation can lead to elevation. Author your life to be a story of success. With everything you do consider answering these questions:

What are your:

Goals? _____

_____

Restrictions? _____

_____

Actions? _____

_____

Decisions? _____

_____

Evaluations? _____

_____

Final Words

I believe everyone is destined for greatness. We are all made with the capabilities and the capacities to achieve success. Although one person's version of success may differ from another person's version, everyone can reach higher and higher. Some people achieve success because they work towards it while others let success pass them by. No matter what success means to you, believe that you can obtain it. Believe that you can strive for perfection. Believe that you can make the GRADE!

CHAPTER 10

Time for the Student to Become the Teacher

The final chapter of this book is dedicated to your legacy. You may recall the tree metaphor that was used in the chapter on resiliency. Part of that tree is the seeds that are left behind. Those seeds are what you teach to other people so that they can grow, too. In this chapter I am encouraging you to share knowledge with other people, especially those that are younger than you.

Although this book covered some crucial topics, there are still more things that you can learn. My main purpose for this book was to get you thinking about these topics as you grow and develop into the extraordinary person you are meant to be. This book was not meant to provide every answer to every question that you may have. Now that you are at the end of this book, please keep in mind what you have read plus the fact that experience is indeed the best teacher. Your life is meant to be lived, so live it to the fullest. Continue to reflect on yourself and what you do. Set your goals, remain positive, treat others better than they may treat you, and sharpen your best skills. The world is yours to shape. Don't just be a game player. Instead, be a game maker. Make things happen for yourself, but remember to be humble and grateful during the process. Your legacy is not only what you accomplish, but also what you leave behind with and for others. Make your legacy lasting and beneficial. Motivate, encourage, and lift up others. After reading this book and having some experiences of your own, you are ready to become the teacher. I pray that you will be the best teacher that you can be. Thank you for reading this book and taking the time to help yourself grow a little more. There's always more work to do and there's always a new level to achieve. Even teachers grow more and more over time. As you teach others, continue to sharpen your skills. As you help others, you are shaping the world one person at a time. Start that chain reaction of helping one person who will go on to help others. After all of this, hopefully you will reflect on what you have accomplished and give yourself a passing grade.

Final Words

Well done! Now, what more can you do? The answer, just like the world, is yours for the taking.

24709762R00046

Made in the USA
Columbia, SC
29 August 2018